Candy,

Last night we spoke of considering an author's perspective. I'm not so sure about the risk or passion generally involved in considering why people portray things the way they do; but by these quotes we have access to the perspectives of those at the apex of our creative society. This is one of my favorite books. I hope you enjoy it.

M. L. R.
MAY 1988

Bliss, Danger & Gods

Bliss, danger & code

SCRIBE & SON   OAKLAND   CALIFORNIA

QVOTES OF RISK & PASSION

Selected and Illustrated
by Sandy Diamond

Scribe & Son
P.O. Box 3612
Oakland, California 94609

First Edition November 1986
Second Edition December 1986

Library of Congress Catalog Number 86-62201
ISBN 0-9617307-0-6

Printed in the United States of America

DEDICATED TO MY PARENTS

ELIZABETH, IN MEMORIAM
AND SAMUEL

WHO GAVE ME BOOKS

INTRODUCTION

This book is an intensely personal anthology, the record of one artist's inner landscape as mirrored in the words of others which she has chosen, and quickened by her own calligraphic art. In *Bliss, danger & gods* an intimate world is made public; it is reminiscent of a dream journal, except that instead of dreams we are given treasured quotes, lovingly, daringly, joyously set forth. They are, as the subtitle tells us, quotes of risk and passion (as well as of quirky humor and surprise) and they are rendered with those same qualities in full measure.

For Sandy Diamond is an artist who is not afraid to take risks. Her cursive brush script — perhaps her most characteristic calligraphic style, the one she uses to bring to life many of her most crucial words and phrases — dips, races and plunges with abandon and authority. Equally powerful are the gestural marks that punctuate the text. "A person's hand is the person" — thus Sandy quotes calligraphy teacher Kazuaki Tanahashi. Sandy's hand is by turns wild and tender, bold and delicate; rarely historical, never stultified, sometimes far from conventionally beautiful but always direct and full of an intense aliveness.

Calligraphy is an odd art form. Perched halfway between the visual and the verbal, it forces us to experience words in a special way — as raw material that the calligrapher can mold and shape for his or her expressive ends. For those whose exposure to calligraphy has been limited to unimaginative versions of "beautiful writing," this book may well be an eye-opener, since

Sandy Diamond's artistic goals are not neatness and prettiness, but immediacy and honesty to the text. While this may be challenging to some, it will surely be visually stimulating as well.

One of Sandy's avatars in this book is Red Riding Hood, walking innocently through the wide world. She will appear several times before the book is through, amongst the bigger, grander texts; and like Red Riding Hood Sandy has strayed from the familiar path to follow the calling of her art. In this she resembles a favorite writer, Gertrude Stein, who ventured far into unexplored territory. Red Riding Hood, Gertrude Stein, and Emily Dickinson (another recurring author) in some sense "carry" Sandy's vision; they embody the unconventionality and courage that she values so highly.

Above all, though, there is an uncompromising quality to this work. It pulses with an integrity and vitality that is uniquely Sandy Diamond's own. She has stayed true to her vision; and paradoxically, while it is utterly personal, it also transcends the personal and touches the universal as well. She gives us her best.

WILLIAM STEWART
San Francisco, July 1986

PREFACE

The first quote I remember was "Hitch your wagon to a star."
Emerson said it first; but for me it came from my father, along
with "Toe out." (But even being pigeon-toed implied that one
could fly.)

These two directives were my travelling companions. I had
my little red wagon, bent toward art; I saw the star in the huge
Ohio sky. How to get there on my wayward feet was the hitch.

In the title of this book, "gods" is used in its original meaning
"what is invoked." As a child much given to reading and
writing and drawing, I invoked the power of words and the
beauty of letters. I watched by my father's elbow as he painted
signs: letters fell out of his brush.

When I first saw the brush writing of Alan Blackman, *his*
wagon (fluorescent pink) was consummately hitched to his star.
I apprenticed myself to that light. His teaching, like his work,
mixed arduous practice with wild speculation, what he calls
"strokes in the dark." Alan warned that good lettering was
"fiendishly hard" and he promised that Daring bestowed
"glories of halos."

The voyage through the Roman alphabet — reading or writing —
is an endless quest; you make up your own map as you go along,
toss it and scrawl another on the back of your hand. The route
is by way of bliss, danger and gods.

SANDY DIAMOND
Oakland, July 1986

GRATITUDES

"...heed thy private dream."

Bliss, danger & gods would still be a sheaf of typewritten pages with graphics taped on it were it not for its inspired designer, Marian O'Brien. Her vision, virtuosity and dauntless resolve were heroic in the face of this *sui generis* combination of typography, calligraphy and visual art.

William Stewart spurred me on, in both major decisions and minuscule refinements quite beyond my slothful wont. Marian's and William's shared commitment to perfection, rendered with loving tenacity, was to my diamond-in-the-rough raw material a treasure beyond reckoning.

The artistry of Don Cushman, founder of the prestigious West Coast Print Center, illuminates each page of *Bliss*. Working with Don — recasting my imagery onto the press's revolutions, scrutinizing together the signatures floating off the rollers — was to be in touch with a master of fine printing.

For the following family, friends and patrons who generously gave encouragement, criticism and/or practical services of help my gratitude is deep: my sister Dianne Diamond, my niece Hilary Diamond; calligrapher-bookbinders Georgianna Greenwood, Jo McCondochie and Lynne Prather; Ruth Gendler, Johanna Goldschmid, Lynda Koolish, Virginia LeRoux and Al Silbowitz, Kris Muller, Kathleen Murphy, Julie Searle, JoAnne Skinner, and Peter Sussman.

Nancy Dickenson and Claire Stroud each offered their art galleries for exhibits in Santa Fe and Berkeley, creating the opportunity for this small volume to be seen in the context of the full body of my work. I thank them for widening heaven.

Because The Friends of Calligraphy created an atmosphere of learning and sharing in both the letter and the spirit of scribal arts, my opportunities for study flourished. Research was facilitated by the painstaking staffs of the Berkeley and Oakland Main Libraries Reference Rooms, who always found one more place to look.

A special bow to my son Gabe who bravely posed with a dinner knife in his teeth for an hour when I needed a pirate. For the countless acts of gallantry and sacrifice demanded of a child all the years of this book, he gets the shiniest medal of all.

Finally, I thank the writers, the artists, actors, dancers, singers, scientists and saints who said it all in the first place. Through the course of finding the way to design their words, I have come to love and honor them beyond words.

sandy

"Delphi...smelled of bliss, danger and gods."

Mary Renault

When much in the woods
as a little girl, I was told that the snake
would bite me, that I might pick
a poisonous flower or Goblins kidnap
me; but I went along and met
no one but

angels . . .

EMILY DICKINSON

1

So Red Riding Hood left the path and wandered off among the trees to pick the flowers. Each time she picked one, she always saw another prettier one farther on. So she went *deeper and deeper into the forest.*

THE BROTHERS GRIMM

2

Little Red Riding Hood was my first love.
I felt that if I could have married
Little Red Riding Hood,
I should have known perfect bliss.

CHARLES DICKENS

Don't ask questions about fairy tales.

"here is god's own delight."

It appears that one day St. Patrick was walking
over the daisy-strewn grass of Ireland on a cliff
by the sea and he saw St. Swithin coming in
a boat. Said St. Swithin, "Is there anything
I can do for you?" "I would delight to have
a bunch of daffodils golden as the sun," said
St. Patrick. Thereupon, St. Swithin reached
over the side of the boat into the sea and
came up with one hundred and twenty three
daffodils for St. Patrick. "Here is God's own
delight," said St. Patrick. "What can I do
for you?" "I would love to have a salmon
from your blessed hands," said St. Swithin.
Whereupon St. Patrick bent down and plucked
a salmon up from the grass and threw it
to St. Swithin.

*"What is the meaning of that story?" I asked my
grandmother. "Wait until you're a hundred years
old and you'll find out," she said. "Everything
doesn't come at once, you know."*

LEONARD WIBBERLY

I like it very well to *change*.

When I *change* suddenly it is very nice

Because if I *change* very suddenly

I do not have to *change* twice.

Once suddenly is better than twice twice.

GERTRUDE STEIN

bbot Lot came to Abbot Joseph and said:
Father, according as I am able, I keep my little
rule, and my little fast, my prayer, meditation
and contemplative silence; and according as
I am able, I strive to cleanse my heart of
thoughts: now what more should I do? The
elder rose up in reply and stretched his hands
to heaven, and his fingers became like ten
lamps of flame. He said:
Why not be totally *changed into fire*?

THOMAS MERTON

9

my fingers

emit sparks of fire with expectation
of my future labours

WILLIAM BLAKE

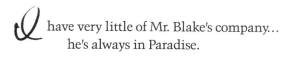 have very little of Mr. Blake's company...
he's always in Paradise.

Catherine Blake

WHEN I DIE AND GO TO HEAVEN

Since colors are seductive, I have learned to
wallow in some of them. The most enjoyable
design that I ever created was an American flag
in the Bicentennial year in which all of it —
the red, the white, and the blue — was done in
fluorescent pink. And of course when I die
and go to heaven, that is how I know I will
be there, because that is the color that
everything will be...

ALAN BLACKMAN

Once her grandmother gave her a little red
velvet cloak. It was so becoming
and she liked it so much that she would
never wear anything else, and so
she got the name of Red Riding Hood.

THE BROTHERS GRIMM

Now I adore my life
With the Bird, the abiding Leaf,
With the Fish, the questing snail,
And the Eye altering all;
And I dance with William Blake
For love, for Love's sake;

And everything comes to One,
As we dance on, dance on, dance on.

THEODORE ROETHKE

13

Fed: Ginger: Fed

You see every once in a while
I suddenly find myself… dancing.

O I suppose it's some kind of an affliction.

Yes, yes… it's an affliction…
I think I feel an attack coming on.

...you know how I love

THE WORLD, WHIRLING GROUSE, GRAMOPHONE RECOR

And at that moment I knew what to send Gertrude and Alice as a house present when I got back to the States.

25 March 1940

My dearest Sammy,
The Mix master came Easter Sunday, and we have not had time to more than read the literature put it together and gloat, oh so beautiful is the Mix master, so beautiful and the literature so beautiful... Alice all smiles and murmurs in her dreams, Mix master

4 April 1940

...perhaps we could write a series of ads for Mix master and get rich that way...

1 May 1940

...the Mix master, Alice just can't tear herself away from the Mix master to tell you how she loves it but she will, it makes spoon bread, it makes mashed potatoes which are a dream...

16

...things that go round...

ND ALL THE REST, ANYTHING THAT GOES IN A CIRCLE."

8 July 1940

Here we are the Mix master and us have all weathered the
storm [the Occupation of France] xcept that just the last day,
Alice dropped the big Mix master green bowl and it fell into
little pieces on the kitchen floor, such lovely green little pieces,
and someday will you send another bowl...

18 November 1940

...alas there is not much to mix these days in the Mix master
but when there will be it would appear that there is a metal
mix master bowl and that we must have, Alice says she would
not like it at all she wants the one she broke she does not want
anything else, we are hoping that mixing will mix soon, you
see you can use other bowls but they do not twirl around in that
lovely green mix master way and when they do not twirl their
contents instead of staying down rise up and spill and therefor
the mix master will have to be a mix master still...

lots of love Gertrude

GERTRUDE STEIN & SAMUEL M. STEWARD

17

The Miller Brothers did their act on board six feet above the stage. "We were doing barrel rolls, trenches and over the tops. We did challenge steps. We had all sorts of novelties, a circular staircase that broke down into three little sets of stairs,

a letter dance.

There's that spirit that makes you do things. The Miller Brothers was an extremely dangerous act. We never thought of it as a dangerous act. We just went up there and did it because that was our thing and we had the feeling for it… You weren't thinking of carrying on a tradition. The only thing that entered your mind was having the best act out there.

HONI COLES

1 merely leap

and pause.   NIJINSKY

in their hearts a kind of dream of divine beauty

While they made beautiful things they [the old scribes] didn't seek beauty directly. They were engaged on serious work. They were writing this kind of writing as fast as they could write an ordinary letter. …they wrote it for their lives and everything they did primarily was for use and even these gorgeous letters they put in their illuminated manuscripts were primarily for use as book markers. Of course they had obviously in their hearts a kind of dream of divine beauty, but at the moment they were doing something that was useful. But note how much of that dream was fulfilled.

EDWARD JOHNSTON

"I am too feeble to go on," says the Wizard
in the Castle bending over his papers at night.
"Faustus!" cries his wife from the bath, "what
are you doing up so late! Stop fiddling with
your desk papers and pen quills in the middle
of the night, come to bed, the mist is on the
air of night lamps, a dew'll come to rest your
fevered brow at morning,—you'll lie swaddled
in sweet sleep like a lambikin—I'll hold you
in my old snow-white arms—

AND ALL YOU DO
IS SIT THERE
DREAMING—"

JACK KEROUAC

Red Riding Hood

picked flowers
until she could carry
no more, and then
she remembered
her grandmother
again.

THE BROTHERS GRIMM

"Never mind about us," Gertrude said, "we'll be alright. The peasants will hide us if necessary. We are just going to set it out, **IT MAY BE DANGEROUS** but we have almost decided that's what we're going to do." "But the pictures in Paris!" I said. "The Germans will take them all!" Gertrude turned almost completely around and even in the dark I could see her wink. "We are going back there secretly if war comes and bundle some of them up and bring them here."
"O my god," I said. "If Paris falls and the Germans find you, they'll kill you for sure. You should just stay here and eat things from your garden." "I had rather be killed for a Picasso than a tomato," Gertrude said.

GERTRUDE STEIN & SAMUEL M. STEWARD

The shore is safer, Abiah,
but I love to buffet the sea —
I can count the bitter wrecks
here in these pleasant waters,
and hear the murmuring winds,

but oh,
I love
the danger!

EMILY DICKINSON

AND I WAS GOING

ᴼ SEA MYSELF

to sea in a schooner,
with a piping boatswain; and pig-tailed
singing seamen;
to sea,
bound for an unknown island,
and to seek for buried treasures!

ROBERT LOUIS STEVENSON

She had found a jewel
down inside herself
and she wanted to walk
where people could see her
and gleam it around.

ZORA NEALE HURSTON

Longing

performs all things.

MARY RENAULT

30

...and I lie in the embrace
    which satiety never comes to sunder.

ST. AUGUSTINE

    This morning I will not
    Comb my hair.
    It has lain
    Pillowed on the hand of my lover.

    HITOMARO

Open your arms.
Take me on your lap.
Sing me a blues.
Be B. B. King to my
Mean woman.

ALICE WALKER

Wild nights
Wild nights
Wild nights should be
futile the winds to
done with the compass
Rowing
ah!
might

ible I with thee
Our luxury!

heart in port,
one with the chart,
n Eden!

he sea!
but moor
Tonight in thee!

EMILY DICKINSON

her soul waz filled with daffodils/
tulips spread in her cheeks

Ntozake Shange

I WILL FOLLOW THEE ALONE,
THOU ANIMATED TORRID-ZONE

EMERSON, *FROM THE HUMBLE-BEE*

no honey for me
nor honey bee

SAPPHO

34

But I that am not shap'd
                    for sportive tricks,
Nor made to court an amorous
                    looking glass,
I that am rudely stamped, and

ωαητ love's ɱajesty

SHAKESPEARE

"Why can't things arrange themselves better?"
"…We don't know what is better. We only know
  things are a kind of crucible, *especially love* …"

RUMER GODDEN

Never, never may the fruit be plucked from the bough
And gathered into barrels.
He that would eat of love must eat it where it hangs.
Though the branches bend like reeds,
Though the ripe fruit splash in the grass or wrinkle on the tree,
He that would eat of love may bear away with him
Only what his belly can hold,
Nothing in the apron,
Nothing in the pockets.
Never, never may the fruit be gathered from the bough
And harvested in barrels.
The winter of love is a cellar of empty bins,
In an orchard soft with rot.

EDNA ST. VINCENT MILLAY

I MAY BE SHIVERING
AT THE FOOT OF
THIS SLOW·GIVING
MOUNTAIN
But the tiny spring flowers
can look / just like you.

FERRON

38

Before my eyes, green mountains —
I have truly loved them.
Why not have their craggy heights
before me every day?

Yuan Zong-Dao

Why cannot the one good
Benevolent feasible
Final dove, descend?

And the wheat be divided?
And the soldiers sent home?
And the barriers torn down?
And the enemies forgiven?
And there be no retribution?...

Under wild seas
of chafing despairs
Love's need does not cease.

STEPHEN SPENDER

40

Very few things happen at the right time,
and the rest do not happen at all;
the conscientious historian
will correct these defects.

HERODOTUS

Never let go
of the fierce sadness
called desire

PATTI SMITH

John Barrymore: You should play Hamlet.

Jimmy Durante: To hell with them small towns,
I'll take New York.

41

One often hears of writers
that rise and swell with their subject
though it may seem but an ordinary one.
How, then, with me, writing of this Leviathan?
Unconsciously my chirography expands into placard capitals.

**GIVE ME A CONDOR'S QUILL!
GIVE ME VESUVIUS' CRATER
FOR AN INKSTAND!**

HERMAN MELVILLE

Small clear chords hung in the air like flowers.
The melodies were like bouquets. There seemed
to be no other possibilities for life than those
delineated by the music.

E. L. DOCTOROW

What has passion got to do with choosing an art form?

Everything.

There is nothing else which determines form.

GERTRUDE STEIN

My feeling about technique in art is that
it has about the same value as technique in
lovemaking. Heartfelt ineptitude has its appeal
and so does heartless skill; but what you
want is PASSIONATE VIRTUOSITY

JOHN BARTH

Ladies & gentlemen
I'd like to do a son
that tells a
that really makes
Awop bopaloobo
Tootie
Al

now
little story
a lot of sense . . .
alop bamboom!
Frootie!
Rootie!

LITTLE RICHARD

I'LL PLAY IT FIRST AND TELL YOU WHAT IT IS LATER.

MILES DAVIS

But, thou, God's darling!

Heed thy private dream.

EMERSON

46

I mean
  that the bells
    that the children
      could hear
        were inside them.

Dylan Thomas

Some people's hills are wooded with
red pine, and some with yellow, and
still not gooseberries; I don't understand it.
I wish I could see a gooseberry bush again;
and an orchard, a very small one, of
quince trees; and a russet apple tree.
If I ever see a russet apple tree, I shall
climb it. And with a book in my hand.
Or, if I find that I must use both hands now
when I climb an apple tree, then

WITH A BOOK IN MY MOUTH

EDNA ST. VINCENT MILLAY

…it is as though one were drawing, one's gaze
bound to the object, inwoven with Nature,
while one's hand goes its own way somewhere
below, goes on and on, gets timid, wavers,
is glad again, goes on and on far below
the face that stands like a star above it,
not looking, only shining. I feel as though
I had always worked that way: face gazing
at far things, hands alone.

RAINER MARIA RILKE

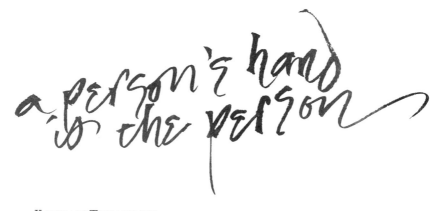

KAZUAKI TANAHASHI

48

I went without discerning
and without other light
except for that
which in my heart
was burning.

UNKNOWN

49

as though somewhere
we were still the children
we once were –

she willed n

the expectant, glad-timid
   Christmas children upon whom
      great surprises descend like angels
         from within and without . . .

RAINER MARIA RILKE

I crept on carpets after her
        as she moved through the rooms
        as tall as wallpaper.
Plaiting my hair and lacing each shoe,
            sewing spurs on my crooked feet,

wings as wide as windows.

SANDY DIAMOND

deep in his act and lost to all around...

on't bring me… some youth who wants
to know what kind of song is likely to win
the crown this year; or what everyone else
is singing, lest he should feel lonely.
…But if you come upon someone who
grabs at song like a child at a bright stone
on the shore, who shapes and re-shapes
like a child building a sand-castle, deep
in his act and lost to all around — then,
never mind if his sand-castle leans sideways,
just give him time. Don't tell him that
this year people are doing, or not doing,
or no longer doing, this or that. Send him
to me, who will… show him the great
shell-beaches and watch him at his play.

MARY RENAULT

53

do not know what I may appear to the world,
but to myself I seem to have been only like a boy
playing on the seashore and diverting myself
in now and then finding a smoother pebble
or prettier shell than ordinary,
whilst the great ocean of truth lay
all undiscovered before me.

SIR ISAAC NEWTON

55

*"YOU LEARN
WHAT YOU NEED TO KNOW
IN ORDER TO SAY
WHAT YOU HAVE TO SAY..."*

"But how do you learn?"
"The way a tennis player learns to play tennis,
 by making a fool of yourself, by falling on your
 face, by rushing the net and missing the ball,
 and finally by practice..."

MAY SARTON

It is necessary always to work.

RODIN TO RILKE

56

To produce lettering is a delicate affair, and it is infinitely excruciating as well. It is a field in which I am a veteran with many wounds.

ERNST SCHNEIDLER

Because she had tarried long in the forest, Little Red Riding Hood had the wolf at her door. She could have been devoured, but just in the nick of time the flower-gathering child gathered her wits about her and slew the slavering beast.

And many years later, she would tell of his eyes, his ears, his terrible teeth, and how she hoodwinked him nevertheless.

SANDY DIAMOND

Artists are healed by their art.

MARY RENAULT 57

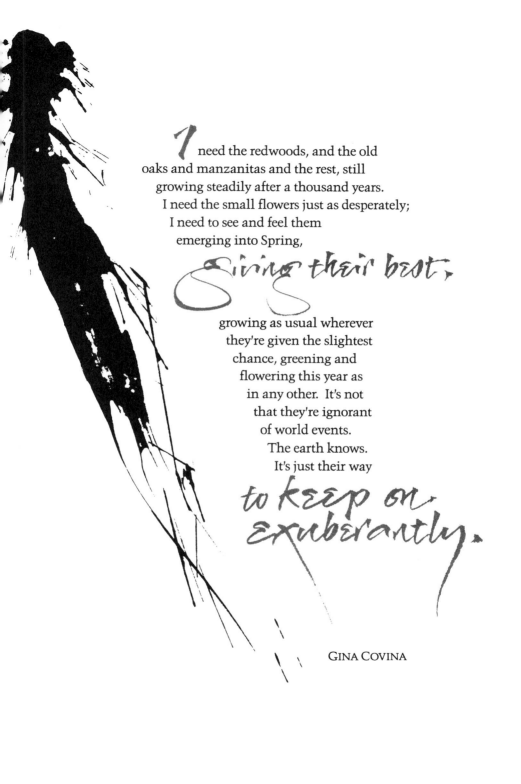

I need the redwoods, and the old
oaks and manzanitas and the rest, still
growing steadily after a thousand years.
I need the small flowers just as desperately;
I need to see and feel them
emerging into Spring,

giving their best,

growing as usual wherever
they're given the slightest
chance, greening and
flowering this year as
in any other. It's not
that they're ignorant
of world events.
The earth knows.
It's just their way

*to keep on
exuberantly.*

GINA COVINA

AUTHORS

FIRST LINES

SOURCES & CREDITS

Astaire, Fred and Ginger Rogers from *Top Hat*, screenplay by Dwight Taylor and Allan Scott. By permission of RKO General Pictures.

Augustine, St. from *The Confessions of St. Augustine*, translated by Rex Warner. The New American Library. © 1963.

Barth, John from *Lost in the Fun House*, jacket copy, by John Barth. Doubleday. © 1968. Reprinted by permission.

Blackman, Alan. *Friends of Calligraphy Newsletter*, Vol. 7 No. 3, from "Friends Or Enemies…Of Calligraphy," by Alan Blackman. © 1982. By permission.

Blake, Catherine and William from "The fiery vision of William Blake is burning bright," by Edward Lucie-Smith, *Smithsonian Magazine*, Vol. 13 No. 6, © 1982.

Coles, Honi from *Cookin' with Honi*, by Ira Steingroot, *The Berkeley Monthly*, © 1978. Reprinted by permission.

Covina, Gina from *The City of Hermits*, by Gina Covina. Barn Owl Books, Box 7727, Berkeley, CA 94707. © 1983. Reprinted by permission.

Dickens, Charles from *Dickens and the Fairy Tale*, by Michael C. Kotzin. Bowling Green University Press, © 1972. Reprinted in *The Uses of Enchantment: The Meaning and Importance of Fairy Tales*, by Bruno Bettelheim. Vintage Books, © 1977. Permission granted by original publisher, Alfred A. Knopf, Inc.

Dickinson, Emily from *The Complete Poems of Emily Dickinson*, edited by Thomas H. Johnson. Little, Brown & Co., © 1960. Reprinted by permission.
The Letters of Emily Dickinson, edited by Thomas H. Johnson and Theodora Ward, The Belknap Press of Harvard University Press. © 1958.

Doctorow, E.L. from *Ragtime*, by E.L. Doctorow. Random House. © 1975 by E.L. Doctorow.

Durante, Jimmy and John Barrymore from *Schnozzola*, by Gene Fowler, Viking Press © 1951.

Emerson, Ralph Waldo from "The Humble-Bee," *American Poetry and Prose* edited by Norman Foerster, Houghton Mifflin Company © 1947.

Ferron, *Proud Crowd/Pride Cried*, from the recording "Shadows on a Dime," by Ferron. Nemesis Publishing, Canada. © 1984. Reprinted by permission.

Godden, Rumer from *In This House of Brede*, by Rumer Godden. Viking Penguin Inc., © 1969 by Rumer Productions, Ltd. Reprinted by permission.

Grimm, The Brothers from "Red Riding Hood" in *Grimms' Fairy Tales*, by The Brothers Grimm. Grosset & Dunlap, © 1945.

Herodotus from *The Histories*, Penguin Books © 1965.

Hitomaro from *One Hundred Poems From The Japanese*, translated by Kenneth Rexroth. New Directions Publishing Corporation, © 1974, 1976 by Kenneth Rexroth. Reprinted by permission.

Hurston, Zora Neale from *Their Eyes Were Watching God*, by Zora Neale Hurston. Harper & Row © 1978.

Johnston, Edward from *Edward Johnston*, by Priscilla Johnston. Taplinger/Pentalic, 1976. © 1959, 1965 by Priscilla Bosworth. Reprinted by permission.

Kerouac, Jack from *Doctor Sax*, by Jack Kerouac. Grove Press, © 1959. Reprinted by permission of The Sterling Lord Agency, Inc.

Little Richard from 1956 telecast.

Melville, Herman from *Moby Dick*, by Herman Melville. Modern Library Publishers, © 1926.

Merton, Thomas adapted from *The Wisdom of the Desert*, by Thomas Merton. Reprinted by permission of New Directions Publishing Corporation. © 1960 by The Abbey of Gesthsemani, Inc.

Millay, Edna St. Vincent from *Letters of Edna St. Vincent Millay*, edited by Allan Ross Macdougall. Grosset & Dunlap, © 1952 by Norma Millay Ellis and by Allan Ross Macdougall.

"Never May the Fruit Be Plucked" from *Collected Poems of Edna St. Vincent Millay*, by Edna St. Vincent Millay. Harper and Row, © 1964 by Norma Millay Ellis.

Newton, Sir Isaac from *Memoirs of Newton, Vol. 2*, by Sir David Brewster.

Nijinsky, Vaslav from *The Family of Children*, edited by Jerry Mason, et. al. Grosset & Dunlap, © 1977.

Renault, Mary from *The Mask of Apollo*, by Mary Renault. Pantheon Books, © 1966. *The Praise Singer*, by Mary Renault. Pantheon Books, © 1978.

The Persian Boy, by Mary Renault. Pantheon Books, © 1972. By permission.

Rilke, Rainer Maria from *Letters to a Young Poet*, by Rainer Maria Rilke, translated by M.D. Herter Norton, W.W. Norton and Co., Inc., © 1954. Reprinted by permission.

Roethke, Theodore from "Once More, The Round" from *The Far Field* by Theodore Roethke. Doubleday and Co., Inc., © 1977. By permission.

Sappho from *The Poems of Sappho*, translated by Suzy Q. Groden. Bobbs-Merrill Educational Publishing, © 1966. Reprinted by permission.

Sarton, May from *Mrs. Stevens Hears the Mermaids Singing*, by May Sarton. W.W. Norton & Company, © 1965 by May Sarton. Reprinted by permission.

Schneidler, Ernst from article in *Graphis* magazine, Zurich.

Shakespeare, William, *The Complete Works of William Shakespeare*, excerpted from *Richard III*. Houghton Mifflin, © 1906.

Shange, Ntozake from *Three Pieces*, by Ntozake Shange. St. Martin's Press, Inc., © 1981 by Ntozake Shange. Reprinted by permission.

Smith, Patti from album cover of "Radio Ethiopia," © 1976 Arista Records, Inc.

Spender, Stephen from "The War God," *Collected Poems 1928-1953*, Random House, © 1955 by Stephen Spender. Reprinted with permission.

Stein, Gertrude from "A Conversation with Gertrude Stein" by John Hyde Preston. From the August 1935 *Atlantic Monthly*, © 1935. Reprinted by permission of Harold Ober Associates, Inc.

Excerpted from "Afterwards" from *Stanzas in Meditation*, by Gertrude Stein, Yale University Press, © 1956. Reprinted by permission.

Stevenson, Robert Louis from *Treasure Island*, by Robert Louis Stevenson. C. Scribner Sons, © 1905.

Steward, Samuel from *Dear Sammy: Letters from Gertrude Stein and Alice B. Toklas*, edited with a memoir by Samuel M. Steward, Houghton Mifflin Company, © 1977 by Samuel M. Steward. Reprinted by permission.

Tanahashi, Kazuaki from *Friends of Calligraphy Newsletter*, Vol. 7 No. 2 "Kazuaki Tanahashi—A Self Portrait." © 1982. Reprinted by permission.

Thomas, Dylan from *A Child's Christmas in Wales*, by Dylan Thomas. New Directions Publishing Corporation, © 1954. Reprinted by permission.

Walker, Alice from "Forgive Me If My Praises" from *Good Night Willie Lee I'll See You In The Morning*, by Alice Walker. Doubleday Company Inc., © 1979. A Dial Press Book. Reprinted by permission.

Wibberly, Leonard from "Two Fables from Ireland," by Leonard Wibberly. San Francisco Chronicle © 1979.

Zong-Dao, Yuan from "For Three Days I Travelled Through Mountains; When the Mountains Came to an End I Was Deeply Moved," from *The Luminous Landscape: Chinese Art and Poetry*, edited by Richard Lewis © 1981 Doubleday & Co.

As a child in Gates Mills, Ohio,
Sandy Diamond drew, painted, lettered
and read. Nothing has changed. She at-
tended Brandeis University and received
a BFA in 1961 from Columbia University's College of Painting and Sculpture
as a Brevoort-Eickemeyer Painting Fellow.
Then she painted. In 1978 she began the
study of calligraphy. Now her daily work
is the painterly writing out of quotations.
She teaches calligraphy, illustration and
design in Oakland, California where she
lives with her son Gabe.

COLOPHON

Bliss, danger & gods was designed
by Marian O'Brien. The type, Trump
Mediaeval, was set by Patrick Miller by
arrangement with Brekas Typesetting
of Berkeley, California. The paper is
Mohawk Superfine; printed by West
Coast Print Center, Berkeley. The
photograph of the author is by
Keith Whitaker.